The Language of Phosphorescence

Poems

Jeff Grieneisen

Lavender Ink
New Orleans

The Language of Phosphorescence
Jeff Grieneisen

Copyright © 2024 Jeff Grieneisen and Lavender Ink.

Printed in the U.S.A.

Book design: Bill Lavender

Library of Congress Control Number: 2024934239
Grieneisen, Jeff
The Language of Phosphorescence / Jeff Grieneisen;
p. cm.
ISBN: 978-1-956921-23-6 (pbk.)

Lavender Ink
New Orleans
lavenderink.org

Acknowledgements

I would like to give thanks to many supportive people in the journey of creating these poems, this book. My first poetry teacher, lifetime mentor, best man, and publisher of MAMMOTH books, Tony Vallone, taught me the finer points of imagery and contemporary poetics, and continues to model poetic and human excellence. Heather Ann Shepard through Tinfoildresses and Jane Carman through Festival of Language provided outlets for publishing and reading my work, both of which allowed me to hone some of the poems you are holding in your hands. I want to thank the late, great H.R. Stoneback for his work in organizing reading opportunities so that some of these poems have been heard by audiences in locales including Paris, Venice, and Ste Marie de la Mer. His lectures and friendship have been an inspiration. Bill Lavender and Nancy Dixon have been solid friends and mentors for many years and have been influential in my work in so many ways, whether by guiding me through my MFA or by hosting the New Orleans Poetry Festival, where some of this work found its genesis and in turn, its audience. John Gery and the Ezra Pound Society have provided opportunities for me to read some of this work in Venice, London, and Philadelphia. I will always also thank Terry Caesar and Eva Bueno for introducing me to the theory and criticism that continues to shape my worldview.

Most of all, I want to thank my family: my loving wife Courtney (Dr. Ruffner) supports me in every way possible, including acting as my greatest critic. Her combination of intellect, strength, wit, and beauty (inside and out) is an inspiration. She is Beatrice to my Dante, a fearless guide and thoughtful partner both personally and professionally. The day we found one another changed my life eternally for the better, and I look forward to every day we have together. My boys, Valentino and Devin, along with his boys Marshall and Ashton, by their very existences, make me want to be a better person. It sounds cliché, but it's true.

I wish to also express gratitude to the following for giving my poems a chance to be read:

"Safety," "The Body," "In Lierna," and "Old Miners" in English, translated into Japanese in *Ezra Pound and Friendship: The Online Fusion of East and West*. Ed. Miho Takahashi. EPIC-Kyoto Committee. 2023.

"Pound, an Understanding"/ "Entendiendo a Pound," "Wasps"/ "Avispas," "My Son Meets a Princess: A Brunnenburg Tale"/ "Mi hijo conoce a una princesa: Un cuento de Brunnenburg" in "*Song Up Out of Spain": Poems in Tribute to Ezra Pound / "Canción desde España": Poemas en homenaje a Ezra Pound*. Ed. Gery, John and Viorica Patea. Clemson UP, 2023.

"Waiting Room," "Young Father Remains," "Jumper," and "The Wasps" in *Tinfoildresses*, ed. Heather Ann Shepard. Spring 2021.

"Sketch," and "The Ring" in *Ezra's Book*. Ed. Kishbaugh, Justin and Catherine E. Paul. Clemson UP. 2019.

"Epigenetics" and "Body and Soul" in *On a Wednesday Night: Poems from the Creative Writing Workshops at the University of New Orleans*. Ed. Kay Murphy. UNO Press. 2019.

"The Opposite of a Kiss," and "The Dead," *Rising in Hope: A Tinfoildresses Anthology*. 2011.

"New Paris." in *Des Hymnagistes: An Anthology*. Lafayette: Des Hymnagistes. 2010

I dedicate this book to the memory of my father, Mike Grieneisen, who died in June prior to the publication.

Contents

The Language of
Phosphorescence

Waiting Room

Old man
alone
Dr. shows him photos
of intestine,
a serpent mottled with a cobra's marking.
They talk low.

Family,
hospital-defiant, loud teenage boy,
tries to change channel from golf,
leaves.   /   Returns,
settles,
peels a muffin
from its wrapper.
Nervous-quiet now.
His mom has a cyst—or a tumor.

She's losing something he can't imagine.

My wife
exhales tiny pieces
of anesthetic, wakes
from behind a curtain
through those doors,
        wakes
back into a world
where she's still whole.

The Word

When did the word become flesh,
       what we call things become the things?
As the Word was God – as in the beginning –
  where was the word
      saying it into existence,
what Cummings called "one / breath
bigger than a circustent"?
Was the word
      abracadabra or some other incantation?

      Who heard the word
that began Everything,
that rolled the hills and mountains, ascending
      the waters—what word made the waves
crash into those white chalky cliffs?
What phrase uttered into existence the billions upon billions
of stars that spin toward some center
we've been seeking for centuries?

What is that mysterious phrase that ignited the bang
       that began it all—that set in motion
all that would become, on a January morning
    of 1970, me?

The word would lead to the earth, to
   the evolution of flesh,
Ichthyostega would crawl onto land,
breathe air, grow fur,
and through one selection after another,
result in my mother and father
meeting outside of Bailey's Drive-In

burger joint,
and on conceiving their third child,
I would be here.

All for a word.

Maybe that word
was "burger" as in "can I buy you a burger, babe?"
or maybe the word was a young tough,
a Fonzie before there was a Fonzie,
showing off for his friends or sharing a malt,
all innocent 50's stuff.

The word might have been a question
my grandfather asked
        my grandmother, requesting
she "accompany" him to the dance
at the Reynoldsville Lodge.
She told me about it only once,
        could not find the words to say
what the dance was for or how he'd asked,

but without that word, my grandparents
never bore seven children, including my mom,
                and without that word
my mom never sneaked away
with my father
        that I could become flesh.

On the Death of My Grandmother

I want it to matter / for generations
that my grandfather lived,
that he built a house for his wife and seven children
from his own hands.

His children now await the man
who will bulldoze the home,
no longer useful,
into a dirt parking lot.

Greedy birds
hold out for the highest bidder,
the one with the most
safflower and millet.

I flattened the few pictures of my grandfather
between the bulge of the bag of sunflower seeds
and the curve of the waste basket
in which my grandmother
kept the sunflower seeds.

If anyone had bothered
to feed the chickadees alighting
on the kitchen windowsill,
as they have done for over fifty years,
they might have found
that photo of grandpa in the straw hat,
squinting into the field
behind the photographer.

Scrub pines have filled in

this old strip mine.
A grove of sumacs
give up fruit that no one knows to harvest,
red cones hiding inside velvet
staghorn antlers of twigs,
long leaves yellowing into autumn
with nothing to show.

Anyone might have found that picture,
clear as the black and white day it was taken,
where my mom and her sisters mocked a rare photo op,
tugging on each of grandpa's arms built strong
by years of turning augers, hammering 2x4's into place,
hoisting shingles up to rooftops for grocery money.

But no one fed those birds,
so I will hang those photos
on the patched and painted walls.
I will spread the seed every morning
scooping out meaning
with the same lavender melamine coffee cup
grandpa used to cloud with a shot of
Pet evaporated milk.

If I stare into that picture long enough,
I'll find some meaning
in the rare genuine laughter,
Swedish hair combed back,
bulging forearms bearing the weight
of a difficult family.

Epigenetics

I. History

Maybe we are the people
of our heritage,
the past distilled
into reaction.

Above the genome,
memories swirl like flocks of birds
seeking entrance, a break,
a way in.
These collected interpretations
survive, enter our bodies
and drill down to our children.
The body is an empty vessel to be filled
with bits of memory, electrical impulses,
or chemicals
encoded on that spiral staircase of DNA,
changing us, forever changed,

and can I feel my grandfather
leaning onto the auger,
drilling a hole in the coal face
to hold the charge.
His hand guides mine
over the open frame of true 2x4's in the cellar.

Scots fled to Ireland fled
to Pennsylvania, USA.
We like to have our heritages,

like inherited yearnings for potatoes
or bad tempers.

Is this where I get the urge to drink? To scratch
out words on these pages?
To tell the stories
as if they've been gathering
in this body for generations?

II. Phobias

Epigenetics Definition: Memories passed down in genes from
    ancestors.

At Emory University school of Medicine,
scientists observe mice
can pass on learned information
about traumatic or stressful experiences
to subsequent generations.
The mouse child or grandchild
does not know why he cowers and runs
from the scent of cherry blossom.

Experiences transfer
brain to genome.
A spider-fright on the boat
from Castaluccio,
and my wife cannot sit beside one,
curds and whey or not.

III. Application

And if we are the people
                of our heritage,

that past distilled,
then am I
cracking the bullwhip,
    calling numbers at auction
sipping tea
        on quiet afternoons?

Are you
    trauma always just below the surface,
learned in generations of broiling sun,
in the field,
        tending to the lifting of things,
or kings
watching boats of rival tribesmen
  cast into the waters
    toward a new land,
        sold into a murky history?

Always double,
    like that helix,
    we cannot forget any sooner
than we could peel our own skin,
    empty that DNA,
dismantled like a de Souza in Benin
    or a Lee
        in Charlottesville.

Night Fishing

Lighting bug galaxy
illuminates the mist
around the lake.

A bullfrog's bellow
drowns the chirp
of a lone cricket.

Minnows sprinkle the moonlit surface.

The maple leans
from my seat
over water.

Black treeline, against gray
sky, melts into its own cloudy
symmetrical reflection.

My line dangles somewhere in a 3 a.m. lake.

Whale Fall

In the places we can't see,
the depths reached with caution
in dive bells,
phosphorescence is a language
more common than our own
and transparency is the only camouflage.

From the window of the vessel
a shower of lights rises,
                              the only evidence
            you are descending.

Somewhere,
      slow descent of tons of blubber

                        and rubbery flesh,

slow motion impact,
      heavy bounce
            raises bits of dust and sand,
the whole body, all limp cold rubber,
                                    then motionless.

Host to an entire ecosystem

                  for decades

Something this big   just died

a field of flesh that was moments ago
                  alive—

The whale leaves behind its body
to be consumed,
        to be a world
that some will know
for generations
as the feast
                of whale fall.

Mobile scavengers begin:
hagfish, sleeper sharks, ratfish
tear soft flesh for two years.
Some live their lifetimes
in this feast, regale descendants
        with the bounty of the old days,
generations feasting on this carcass
in the mile-depth darkness,
the floor where no human
                footprints have furrowed.

Worms and crustaceans
eat leftover blubber
two more years.
Then, a hundred more,
                this field is a bacterial mat
        for mussels, clams, limpets, sea snails,

the body broken down in stages,
                to dust it shall return
by crab or eel, by bacteria.

And the very phrase

"whale fall"

sounds gentle as the whale, itself,
drifting downward, last breath exhaled,
now drowned
        in the secret medium of its existence,
returned to the world,
      a world unto itself and others.

Poem from a Jumper

Most people don't live long enough
to inhale water.
There is no drowning

at the foot of the Golden Gate Bridge,
but there are fractured ribs
almost every time, almost every rib,
as if Adam himself could be shattered.

Shards of bone travel like tiny scalpels,
haphazardly pierce the spleen, the liver.
Shattered vertebrae seek organs
like search missiles.

One woman jumped from Golden Gate,
second trimester pregnant,
with no injury to the uterus or fetus,
as if someone held this baby
in large, soft hands.

Midway

We should die
before we can feel
our child
torn from his lover,
she running her hand along his chest,
he winning her a stuffed tiger
at the fair.
They will outgrow this
and learn to hate each other's slurps,
crunches of toast,
the infinite future lost
to the reality of pushing a stroller
along a highway.

Forever is not a long time
but a temporary idea
in the annual, small-town fair,
kids spinning in tilt-a-whirls
or shuffling hand in hand through the junk
of novelty t-shirts or long feathers on roach clips,
eating greasy fries and hot sausages
and deep fried things.
Once grown, they will go to work,
one-day-a-week off,
maybe a week's vacation.

Until then, we know them
by the angle their heads make,
tilted toward one another,
making a peak, head to head,
as if tomorrow will never come.

They love as if love is all they need.
They could fall asleep right here.
Now.
Forever.
Lost in one another.

We've all been there,
felt like the next moment
doesn't exist—will never occur
because we have this. Now.
But we need to pay rent, car insurance,
and when the fair comes to a close,
we pull our fingers apart,
take our hand out of our lover's back pocket,
forget the barker's call,
and rejoin the world.

Sketch

She woke
to the near-finished sketch
of herself
sleeping
in the hostel
on top of *Montmarte*,
the last lines
on her fingers
curled, unseen
under her chin.

She stretched
beneath scratchy sheets
before we all had to leave
for the day,
the staff
stripping bunk beds,
wiping down communal showers.
Another day in Paris,
another metro ticket,
another café dialog with waiters:
Jambon? Oui, Jambon.

Another day of skipping
Louvre lines,
peering into houses
of the dead
in *Pére Lachaise*,
adorned with inconsolable angels,
bronze men breaking free,
cottages of small stools and brooms.

We found the famous residents:
Morrison and Stein,
Chopin and Proust,
Wilde.

And *La Rive Gauche, Montparnasse,*
eternal homes of Baudelaire, Sartre,
de Beauvoir, de Maupassant
where we felt we belonged.

We met the Norwegian sketch artist
on a closed Sunday evening,
all of us dragging luggage around *Calais* for hours.
He gestured "I know a place in Paris."
We'd nowhere else to go.

We slept in that hostel
among friendly strangers,
cheap nights in strange beds.
Our last night, the innkeeper
bought us Heinekens from the vending machine
as tuition to practice his English with us.
I don't remember what we talked about,
just the quick morning *au revoir.*

Still, she sleeps
on that thick paper shoved
between brochures of Tower Bridge
and the Vatican, always between cities,
where she replays that summer,
her memory
forever wandering.

Young Father Remains

His smile, parentheses
drawn from the corners of the nose
arced down,
                    ending
parallel to his mouth
                         like gills

Sudden lost weight
leaves creases like
the organ
of filaments that cannot breathe air,
or the interlude
of an afterthought

GoFundMe
runs out,
medical bills
and insurance statements
tucked into a basket
on the countertop
to be gone over
                    sometime later

Digital account
           active
as if he will post
another picture
                    with his daughter
wading
into a stream
that looks cool on the page

maybe stopping again
for a coffee
selfie with barista
selfie of the coffee

heart in foam

His boy too young
        to remember him
his mother will tell
her stories, and the photos,
all digital, many posted already,
will tell their own story

In this photo
a realization
                no afterthought
eyes focused inward
no smile

He is away
from the children,
they on the left, he
on the right

as if
he knows this experiment
will not work

Where I Notice It

Parentheses
around the mouth
those lines
that weren't there
show through
slow chewing.

Something's missing,

some heft
over top teeth,
some matter
around the cheekbones
now so well defined,

something in the eyes
pleading
with time, with destiny,
some glimmer
dimmed into a fear.

Slowly resigned
to small food,
quiet walks
to the bathroom
finger running over the ridges,

erosion takes
the subtle fatty layers
and
eventually
leaves
nothing.

Parkland

Two hundred miles
northwest,
my own son
safely tucked
behind the iron fence
keeping danger out
and the bullies in,
he kicks
a red ball
to his buddies
on the playground outfield.

If I think about it
I might quake
for the parents
who do not have the safety
of this distance,
who are on their way
right now,
praying on this Ash Wednesday
that they will not return a human
to the earth today,
that their son or daughter
is not ash,
that they will not
wait outside
of the large swinging doors,

slump in chairs,
nurse bad coffee
brought in stages
by people who need to move
to support.

Their fears echo
outward, upward,
as the drills push our children
behind the tape lines on the floor,
teachers making games
with prizes for quiet
in dark classrooms
to stifle elementary giggles.

Cosplay shooters terrify children
the same as a real one,
no fence too high
for the revolving
guidelines, to shelter,
to hide, to run, to cry,
and to do it all silently
so as not to die.

In Memoriam, Crocodile Man

for Harold Nugent

They gather
on these pages of digitized, pixelated photos
from long-obsolete cameras,
each a celebrated pioneer member
of the International Union
for Conservation and Nature.

Christian de Coune poised
behind the "international association of falconry" sign,
just printed on the cardboard
folded into a conservationist name plaque
at some convention,
maybe in his own Hungarian town.
His thick, black eyebrows combed back like wings.
Gray hair meets a neat beard that frames his serious
    expression,
pen poised to jot down some point
of breeding or toxicity.

Welsh cycad specialist Ken Hill, distant, bespectacled,
exiting the woods beside one of the trees he considered
    children,
hippie safari hat, Grizzly Adams beard, camera hanging from
    his neck.

They keep time on the page, with Harold,
the New Hampshire linguist
and Crocodile Man,

always with a warm smile,
and the gentle lisp of a New Englander
who softens his language
into non-Rhotic* diphthongs
to offset the terrible snows of winter.

At the regional English conference, he could find no more
    comfort
in human language and was drawn deeper into the swamps,
following the crocodilian bellows, taking out small ones
with taped jaws for school children to pet.

Long done with the variables of human clicks,
glottal stops and alveolars,
he sought the bellows and oxymoron
of the ancient familiar creature.

---

*   *a non-rhotic speaker "drops" or "deletes" the /r/ sound*

The Body

Body implies a mass, a heft in air,
a discovery.

Infants have no awareness
of body until the object permanence stage
at 15-24 months as rogue tests show.
Rogue, as if self-awareness is savage or destructive.

When we put our body, itself 65% water,
into a lake, we can float
if we've learned to balance ourselves
on the tension of that surface.

Yet 3,533 people each year quietly sink
beneath the blanket
of surface. Lungs, that tiny portion of air in our bodies,
fill, eyes gaze into some new light.

Drowning is not the cinematic thrashing
but a slipping in,
a deceptively quiet event.
A drowning person instinctively presses down
                    on the surface,
arms lateral, not up high.
                There is no waving,
only failed swimming.

A pond or lake, even an ocean,
                seems to sit still, like a body.
A river is fluid motion, lacks heft or definition,
        lacks the stasis of defined boundaries,

always replacing itself with what's upstream
like the constant renewal of skin cells.

Our own bodies are in constant motion, replacing
      cells by the billions, passing waste, walking, or running.
We call ourselves a body,
but what it is that inhabits that body?
What soul or spirit, what eternal energy is confined
      by the border of flesh,
    tiptoeing out at night or further inward?

Science attempts to measure the energy that leaves
the body upon death, something that can be weighed
to prove its existence, since *to be* is to have
presence in air—to have heft—to become real.
If this energy has weight, then the soul
      can have mass, and so, be.

We have a Mass to sing about the lost,
to celebrate the soul to heaven,
to know that whatever the being was or is, is not
      in the body left in that coffin or on that stage.
It has ascended from the lake or river,
from the body with a broken head at the bottom of the staircase
or from the supine corpse in bed.

The body we know will be sealed
in cement casing
and inside, a wooden box, all measured to perfect dimensions,
buried to a depth of more-or-less 6 feet.
The body, we learn, returns to dust,
the stuff of the mass
of the universe we are all part of.

If the soul is energy and has heft, it may keep itself
from others, whether massless photons or charged electrons,
to not blend into a mosaic of all-souls,
finally converging in some huge waiting room,
each waiting for another's arrival.

My Son Meets a Princess: A Brunnenburg Tale

She blows a hoot through the ocarina
of her clasped fingers, and they share
a wide-eyed laugh
at the top of the castle.
He rounds his mouth
to show his own hooting whistle practice
then pumps the rocking-horse back and forth
in the library of her own grandchildren
she's preserved for visitors like us.

Pound said "make it new"
        and Mary says we made it new with Valentino
as Pound made it new with her.

She hopes he will keep our old traditions
        as she keeps her father's legacy
but moves forward step by step,
climbing that mountain every day
into town for small essentials.

Oh, to be a Pound in a world of new terrorism
        and New Deals laid out on senate tables
where the young are still sent to slaughter,
and this skipping, whistling boy shines into every corner,
laughs easily, and just wants to keep digging
with toy cars into Northern Italian slopes.

Cradle

The emptiness hovers over us
like the souls of twin babies
rising somewhere to a purgatory
where their uncles wait.

We try to empty sorrow
from our eyes,
lean into one another
before she even puts on
her pants—one leg at a time.

The room is sterile beautiful.
I sit in the corner chair,
the sonographer talking
in clips. The doctor, a blue ghost,
materializes

to ease sharp news
onto us like a pillow, the words
inflating like red balloons,
a thin surface over emptiness.

And when the dilation is complete
and the suction and scraping done,
we're left again,
now at home, just us,

holding each other
tightly to squeeze out
the emptiness.

Jumper

They found
not a ripple in the water
where she'd plunged
    430 feet,
but her car consumed in flames
on that bridge
that the happy call *Sunshine Skyway*.

A 12-hour search for the body ended
with remains turned over to the medical examiner.

James Dickey romanticized a stewardess's fall
    from an airplane, immortalized her in verse
as if she'd somehow found salvation in that plummeting.

I do not think Meg found solace
but accelerated at 32 feet per second each second
after she stopped her car at the height
of that span with the beautiful name,
launching her plan to make some statement
    that no one knows.

Maybe it was an impromptu drive over the bridge,
a sunny 11 a.m. commute,
matches and a quart of lighter fluid or gallon of gasoline
conveniently on the passenger seat,

her last act, a fiery performance piece
that we might interpret

if we knew whether she jumped
nervously, feet first, or dove?

Time

Instant chaos of time
greens the pool straining
through a filter, breaks hydrogen
from oxygen   lifts these into air
as they hover above the water,
are carried away   into the breeze
and stick to new-sprung leaves.

Each season   a leaf
draws the tree closer
to falling, rotting from termites,
dry rot, blackened age   through the roof
made of an old tree like this one,
a tree that never fell   on its own.

The chaos of time bows this old roof,
sagging toward   the center
of the house's earth.   Cracks along the wall
open as the ground fills in spaces
beneath it that the earth can't   ignore.

With no time, the house
could hover   over spaces—
there would be no forever
wings to enfold the walls and shingles
to make it last. It sags   like an aging person
every step, unable to earth its own roots
and lie   against gravity—
gravity, we know, that speeds time
against our wishes.

Patent Pending

Once in a bar, I forget the name, I talked to a man who gazed into me and stammered—looking over my shoulder—*I once had a great idea that those living in low latitudes did not develop intellectually as those who had to adapt to climates to heat indoor space and wear sweaters* and he said that he had an idea that AIDS has directly caused the *leveling off of divorce despite rising domestic violence* and he could deduce pi to some impressive degree. But all his systems, all his ideas, *were stolen by professors at graduate school.*

And when he went to the bathroom, I took a cigarette from his pack.

In Lierna

We sit amid this after-work crowd,
drafts pulled hastily into glasses,
burnt pizza carried to our table.

Ruffians drink small beers,
bar maid shoos flies off tapas
with an old fly swatter,
sometimes knocks the ham from thin bread,
and puts it back
without shame.

After Postmodern Question

White smoke rises
from butt-ends of Marlboros,
one left-over oyster cracker
limps in humid air,
a pinned insect
scratches the balsa wood floor
in the cigar box.

I fashion myself a prude
against the swelling sea of voices
wandering through Wal-Mart
aisles at 11 p.m. or 1 a.m.
I wonder when my head will be served up,
when I'll learn to ask the questions
that need to be asked.

Before they choose the carts,
load the merchandise
of one-night-only cheap-stuff racks,
there is smoke
rising into drifts
like evaporating wreaths,

scattering into the questions
we all have, overwhelming questions
that lead us to new leaders,
frightening mirrors
against which we appear silent.

The Magnificent Story of Brooke

She of the rare disease
never will age past a toddler,
loves to be tickled and cuddled,
serves DNA
for scientific inspection
to unlock the secrets
of not-aging,
a chance at immortality.

We might wish for that
chance to hold our toddlers
for twenty years,
forego the eye-rolling teenage moods,
the worry that you'll get the call
from a state trooper,
summoned to identify,
witness the blossoms of metal,
what speed does to machines
and bodies.

What lengths we go
to preserve the smiles
of innocence
untouched by the knowledge
that makes us sad,
that can never be forgotten,
untouched by experience
that shows us the suffering
of earth.

Coming Home

That car did not swerve
into my lane. It wobbled a moment
then recovered.

A man I don't know from my hometown
ran his motorcycle
headlong into an 800-pound elk,
was pronounced dead at the scene.
At 6 a.m.
52 years old.

Any of us could die in that instant,
red light runner, daytime drunk driver,
almost always in a car.
But something could fall from a roof,
a baby grand, for instance, like in the cartoons,
crush us into an accordion.
It might be simpler,
an amoeba in the sand, an escalator, an aspirin.

But the highway is also the place of miracles
every day you return home
unscathed by road rage shootings, carjackings at red lights,
or sleepy commuters. Every day you kiss your wife,
your son running into your arms,

both glad you're home,
neither expecting you not to be.

Sounds of Parenthood

Mommmmm mummmmm
The sound
easy m's
the humps like upside-down breasts
the lip smacking hum
of satisfaction,
like a musical note all one tone
vibrating lips with voice
first words, more maternal, mammary
than dad. D d d d d
"du" "duh" like a violence,
the tongue flicked to the roof of the mouth
pushing a tiny shaft of air outward
and away from the body,
Dad. What the boy says:
 "dads dads daddy,"
The "y" trying to soften it all up.
Dad. Da. Pere.
The French use "p," still pushing air
from the body, but sounds like Pear
the fruit shaped like a woman.

Mére maman, mutter, or madre, it's all mmmmm
Pére and papa,
Vater like water,
the life force of womb home
which has nothing to do with father,
or Vader an evil father or a drowning
in dryness.

My Name

Never pronounced the same way twice
I don't correct unless asked
"Is this right?"
I get Gren, like Grendel
A soft sound for a monstrous person-like
giant.

Some insist on a nonexistent "h" as in "heisen"
like an uncertain principle
or a calmer "hi, zen" or "high zen."

Eye-zen
would be right
(without the h),
a way of seeing enlightenment,
a seeing of seeing.

Old German for iron, eisen,
and Grien, now called grün,
green,
forged from
liquid metal, the green iron of steel
that would build
Pittsburgh, town of my father's people,
my own past assembled and fabricated.

A Kind of Regret

My uncle's gurgling
rhythmically descended into night,
hovering over the gray trees
beside the window.

In the next room, I held my breath
so I could hear anything irregular.
Sometimes, he woke
and I emptied the urinal bag
strapped to his bed-rail.
Then we talked about when he was young.

He told me again about his racecar trophies,
raising hell with Becker and Smitty,
and how a little Vietnamese girl warned him
not to eat the big bugs with orange legs.

One night, in a tone
lower than usual, he told me about a plane
he fixed. *I was crew chief mechanic, you know?*
He watched from the base as the plane fell
into the village like a hatchling
kicked from the nest unable to take wing.

He, too, is dead now.
I wasn't there to hear his last
deep, rattling breath.
I couldn't go to bury him, either,
but sometimes when I think of that night
I remember he told me he hated Florida—the last place
he knew I was alive.

I hope he knew that I made peace
with the swamp
and that he didn't spend his last day
replaying the horror
of that plane—the one that got away—
his own breath fading
into the early morning dark.

The Truth About Blackberrries

for Galway Kinnell

I pulled jaggers from bare legs and clothing,
covered my eyes against the brittle sun,
then it was time for business,
back to the old routine: filling
quart buckets, juice pitchers,
filling kettles and pans with ripe blackberries.

Picking out stink bugs that hide
with army ants and aphids beneath drooplets,
I pluck these strong and tart berries from the bushes
in one piece, unlike sweet, weak red raspberries
that fall apart in your fingers,

stain you with the sin of theft
from birds and deer. A thousand other animals need
the berries more than I need jam. I don't need any more
berry syrup or berry wine,
but I still forage through briars,
consumed by this obsession
to empty the bush of its berries.

Soon, the sting of the berry juice saturates
pin-holes left in my fingertips,
and when the birds aren't looking,
I lick my fingers to clean the bloody stains.

Seed

What is it about snakes
that makes my love scream?
Like a long, reptilian penis of an animal.
that swims through grass and trees.

I thought I saw a snake in the pond
behind our house,
but that was an Anhinga, a magical bird
that knows how to swim, pretends to be a fish
beneath the water's innocent surface.

What do the fish care? They're just trying
to find the worm without the hook, to live
another day. I can't imagine
the ultimate moment, private, underwater,
as the Anhinga digs a sharp, hooked beak
into the silent fish that twists
its head & tail
back & forth.
What else could it do,
betrayed by such a beaky grin?

Maybe that's what it is with snakes, too.
They seem innocent enough: smooth, sleek,
almost watery, but beneath their sheen,
under their armor, is a fork-tongue
creature who lies to get his way, who lies
to see Eve take the fall, who lies
so like the phallus he resembles,
to spread his venom
into one more wound.

Led Astray

Caught on film today,
a grainy man behind City Car Wash
led a girl away. Without sound,
we saw him talk to her,
tell her something we might believe,
your mother's hurt or *your father asked me*
to take you.
At what point do we stop believing
in the kindness of strangers?
Maybe the buck stops here—where
Amber Alert has nothing to do
with terrorists
and everything to do with a young,
smiling man leading a girl away
to a cabin, perhaps, or a truck
grinning up I-75
or I-4 across the state.

We Owe Our Lives to the People We Love

If we damage ourselves enough, people
who reach out to feel our missing bits of flesh
notice parts that are no longer there.

I think of this when I drink too much
or when I wonder if my mother could smell
damp smoke clinging to my clothes and hair.

This cold day reminds me
of every funeral I've attended
and that nearly everyone I knew who died,
died in spring,
as if after a hard winter, they said *enough*.

What would the flag of my death look like?
It might need green,
like my grandmother's vast front yard
and the weeds that grow just beyond it,
or gray for the coal dust settled deep into her cellar walls
and her piece of sky.

I lived there too.
I have gray dust in my skin.
I inherited gray dust in my veins from my grandfather
and his father. Both clawed black nuggets
from Allegheny Mountain hillsides
until spring.

Meaning in the Park

An ant is the crumb of life.
Water is the fire of heaven.
Twelve men are a jungle of dreams.
Trees stand against the presidency of clouds.
Tomorrow is a song I've already sung.
The green shadow of a leaf falls and rises
in the blue air of summer wind.
On the wooden park bench, the young couple
argues over the meaning of grass.
Smoke from the distant power plant clusters
into animals waltzing offstage.
A rock is the sage of history,
the smallest pebble, a stream of hidden knowledge,
a stone, the lonely daybreak this morning.

The Wasps

This morning's sun breaks
cold sleep.

Frozen lives begin
again.

With silent wings they lift
from mud,

legs hang
like landing gear.

They entomb larvae
in the secret spaces

of paper
houses.

Morning Ritual

We face ourselves
foggy and drizzly
in the beaded, split images
of our mirror.

The sink clogs again with old toothpaste
and the long hair we insist on growing.
Swirls of dust gather in the corners
of dull faucets.

You test the curl of your hair
against a moist palm.
It springs back.

I refuse to shave
because I can't sweep all my beard-ends into a pile,
and you don't want me to try
because last month you spent weeks
gathering traces of me from the crevices.

So this morning we'll pull dress shirts
and slacks from smooth, plastic hangers,
face the mirror before the fog lifts,

and leave the house
locked safe until evening
in the silence of morning.

Understanding by the Pound

Words echoed from the furthest reaches
    of humanity,
"Pull down thy vanity"

We read these tales
    echoed and retold

       nothing gold
can stay
but we have these
    tales in ourselves
built into
these stories of biblical men and women

greek stories
of goddesses gone
to underworlds
for a brief time
    stories of reflections in Venetian pools
streams running stagnant
under beautiful bridges
and beneath old, sanctimonious churches

and we breathe deeply
and usher forth cries
"beauty is difficult"
"art is beauty"
therefore
art is difficult
life is difficult

how do we order from the German waiter
off this Italian menu

how do we walk the vertical cliff
into the town that sleeps by day

learn our rules
from weathered cliffs
and silent stone castle walls
and the chatter of children
learning the rules
of ideograms,
of sharing
eggs
in the
morning
and wine in the evening

once a week, we carry egg shells
and coffee grounds and peels
to a pile by the barn
and the vineyards whisper
their own secrets: the old woman watches
from an unseen window
the town watches
from its own kind of window

and above it all,
we study the words
we can't read
we read the words we can't
understand
and we understand

that sometimes
it's okay
to just
read the goddamn thing

The Opposite of a Kiss

A kiss is a touch or a brush or sometimes just a gesture
from across a room, crowded or empty.
Kiss-and-tell, baby kisser, kissing cousins.
Kith and kin?
Kiss your ass goodbye, kiss this,
kiss my grits.

Kissing is violent
like a smack, a reminder:
smack your forehead, smack down
this smacks of something else.
If a butterfly can kiss a dandelion,
it can also smack a dandelion.
A smack on the lips is a kiss
or the harsh hand of an angry mother
when you talk back.
Smacking your lips is a kiss
in the air, a kiss that misses
the target.
So tonight, love, please be patient,
and smack me until the morning's purple.

The Ring

I twist this ring
into the pale groove it's left
after only six months.
I'm no more able to live

without it as I am able to sit
without my wallet pressing into
spaces made familiar.
If I could stand naked
I would still need to feel this band,

to spin it while I think of words
when I'm not sure what words to use.

As there is no weight to a knuckle
that exists only where two bones meet,
there is no weight to the center
of this ring, a space between our souls.

Particles of gold scratch off
by stone walls and iron railings,
float through our honeymoon cities
Frankfurt, Munich, Vienna, Trentino, Dorf Tirol.

Bits smaller than dust
lost to the ground will resurrect,
find a way to band together again
or remain lost forever
among the shifting earth.

Bird

Too young to call out, too weak
to open bulging, blue-black eyes,

it clawed the air
with a fragile yellow beak,
stretched
and folded tiny naked wings.

Busy, angry ants gnawed
a dead sibling clean to skeleton,
tugging at flesh,
snipping pinfeathers,
mandibles grasping at black bones.

I built a grassy nest
in the Buster Brown box
to keep the live bird under the hutch
where a desk lamp glowed warm.

A primal and innocent scent
of small flesh, and tiny bird poops
littered the grass I couldn't clean.

Mealworms from the pet store
in clear plastic containers of oatmeal
and eyedroppers of sugar water
were never enough.

No human
mothering or fathering
could bring this knot of veins and flesh
through to feathered flight.

I buried the whole box
in a hole I dug behind the garden,
marked with a stick
I drove in as hard as I could,
laid a dandelion on fresh dirt.

Soon I moved on to praying mantises,
skinks, and turtles by the creek.
And there would be other baby birds,
all buried behind the garden or beneath
the yew just beyond the yard.

The Dead

We protect them from rain and worms,
cradle their heads in satin,
dress them to the waist
in suit jackets.
One last look
so we can tell ourselves
that we will not diminish—
we will look alive
with rouge, powder, cobbler's thread,
our withered hands clutching
a satin sheet.

Stephen Dunn tells us that the living
were sometimes buried
by accident or scheme,
scratching deep trenches
into the insides of coffin lids.
Fools were hired to test the body,
pull the tongue, strings connected
ring fingers of the doubtful dead
to bells at ground level
for the graveyard shift.
Victorians buried their dead
in safety coffins
with window views
and air supplies.

The coffin is a house
of last rites, a house of descent
into which we all fall,
even the cremated, ground to powder

at a forge—blended into the only ash
that should be wiped onto our foreheads.
Then the world does its work,
and we are left out of our own stories.

The Numbers of Marriage

We think
of those things we don't want to think about—
our house vacant for a month,
how the numbers will add up
to "two" to "one"
mortgage, power, and water,
recurring numbers
we write onto blank checks
every month.
Where is love? The shoe
in the gut wiggling its toes
that defies numbers, that speaks
with its forked tongue, unlacing
the
          proper order
of things.

Where do the numbers fall into
the great scheme of things:
napkins, match books,
postage necessary to the language
of love—numbers spoken as words
important as "three" to trinity.
We fill in lines of our thin checks
spelling out the numbers,
crossing the "t" in "three" carefully
so it's not confused
          with any other language

Fetish

Her delicate head turns
easy in my cupped hands.
Petroleum fumes rise
from her smooth-perfect flesh.
She smiles but does not blink.
Tight dress falls away from her body.

I suck on her arching toes.
Kisses linger to the bare
flesh between her legs. My scissors cut
through air. I groan "you want it"
snipping blond locks.
Shorter. Shorter. Shorter.

Her fuzzy head is smeared with Gillette.
I sharpen my blade.
The last clumps of blond fall
onto my naked lap. Her bald head gleams
like oiled flesh. The last streaks
of shaving cream I licked carefully from the blade
slide under my tongue.

I raise her arms and scissor her legs
to please me. She would squeal
if she could. But she is helpless.
I control her. Barbie's head flattens
between my thumb and forefinger
until I twist it from its neck.

It slides like an egg
down my throat.
I am an aroused shudder.

The Birds Repeated Warnings

The birds repeated warnings
in the shrill voices of lost children.
I sat by the pool, listening to cockroaches
crying like crickets against November.

The veteran's hand-crank
hospital bed perches
in the corner of the living room
like a wounded heron,
its bent leg stuck out as if it survived
some strange accident.

I gather up the butts I used
to count the day's descent
from where they landed, one flick
away from the porch,
so I can go in, pause
before the empty space.
Maybe I'll pray
for the first time in a long time,

and I'll plan to visit the cemetery,
to scratch out a space
with a trowel so anyone can plant
peonies, chrysanthemums, or violets.

All the while, starlings repeat
the warning cries of fallen soldiers.
They seem to call me from my planting.
I follow their warnings to the tree line
beside the cemetery, where they fade

like black snow into the twilight of the woods.

I wonder if I'll ever make it back to the cemetery,
if I'll ever scrape away that clay and mud
so that anyone can fill the space with color.
It's been a long time already, and I'm still sitting
in the front yard next to the sumac
where dark birds peck seeds
from the red clusters of soft berries.

Tomorrow I will go. Yes, tomorrow
I must donate that bed to AmVets
so the space in the living room
can be used for something else.
Until then, I must count days
and listen to the warnings of birds
who know better than I do
how to make the day end.

Bad Students

They wish they could ride motorcycles
to school. They wear scuffed boots
and sunglasses indoors,
sway in their sets in the back of the room.
When we read stories about teenagers
they close in on their books;
their eyes open. Today we watched
Greasy Lake—one boy took off his sunglasses
to see tits onscreen in the classroom, the torn shirt
of the woman three 19-year-old boys almost raped.

He shared the story of his own Greasy Lake,
the secluded beach
at North Island Point. Now it's ecstasy
and pot—nobody huffs paint or gasoline
anymore, nobody has sniffed glue
since the 70's. But it all comes back.
Model airplane glue safe as Elmer's school paste.

In elementary school, we thought he was bad
when Jay turned his eyelids inside-out
or ate a soup of three foods stirred together
during a lunchtime boy's dare.

In high school, we wore Levi's denim jackets and shades.
Our Greasy Lake was the pool pavilion
called Garb Island,
cigarette smoke, tiny bags of weed
hidden in our pockets
or funneled into cleaned-out cigarettes,
Led Zeppelin t-shirts, stringy hair.

Through the chain link fence we watched
girls whose parents bought them annual pool passes.

One day a van pulled up,
offered us free food, all we wanted.
We rode along to a tent that was alive
with singing, then quiet with solemn
tones of brimstone.
Hardcore Jamie, the baddest pavilion head,
all zits and dangling earrings
and some home angst none of us knew,
closed his eyes against the rhythm of the Words,
        come up, my children
and Jamie swayed
            come up and be Saved
and Jamie
clenched his eyes like fists,
        come up, come up
and Jamie slumped
to the front,
kneeling
in the line-up,
saving himself
in the name of all us greasy, pimpled boys
who had been taken.

Black Scar

The black scar of earth
over the obsidian vein runs
beneath the house my grandfather built.
So rich was the earth he opened
the cellar floor—tunneled into coal
and sold pick-up loads
to Appalachian farmers.

When his joints ached and
he melted into the dusty sofa,
my grandmother went to work
at BF Goodrich
making golf balls out of rubber bands
for rich people in Florida country clubs.

Every day, my grandfather creaked
to the cellar door, peered
into the darkness when the cellar filled
with rain water.
Years later, even if he could descend
the wobbly stairs,
the shaft he hand-shoveled had collapsed,

so he shuffled back to the sofa
until whatever-it-was-he-had cleared up.
He worked with Amish carpenters,
always a handshake away from his next paycheck,
laid the floors in the local tavern,
shingled the roofs of depression-era housing
that dotted the countryside,

worked until the day he died.
My uncle found him, still alive,
at the bottom of the stairs,
where the brain hemorrhage
laid him down.
The mortician's powder covered his scars
like jimsonweed grew to hide the house.

Angels' Wings

Grandpa told me that candles
are angels' wings. We
burned one every year, a thin white taper
singed like the pinion of a dove,
on the day that he died.

When I was little I was afraid
the candle would bring him
from where he was, a place
I didn't know.

The white candle
burned like a wish, or the secret
an angel tells you before he presses
a hushed dimple over your lip
(a poet once told me that).

Otherwise, we lit a single candle
only when the wind blew out our power.
Mom fumbled through our kitchen
junk drawer, cursing the corkscrew and stray tacks.

But then we weren't huddled silently around it,
thinking of grandpa's big black shoes
caked with garden dirt, or him pulling and pushing
the choke on his tan Nova.

One day I'll shut off the breakers
on the day grandpa died,
light the half-burned candle
with a strike-anywhere Blue Kitchen match
      and watch until its last wisp of smoke
trails upwards into darkness.

Left Holding

Today, the baby almost died.
They tried for years to conceive the perfect child.
She counted her lunar cycles, ate mangoes,
checked her temperature twice a day, even prayed

to a god she didn't believe in.
When her egg finally divided
they bought a new house,

finished the baby's blue room first
with a new, plastic bassinet, monitor,
chunky books, the secret, cliché football.

She grew a day late, a week late.
All their worries resolved in a seeming ocean
rushing toward Maternity Ward East.
Concerned doctors sliced her warm belly,

lifted her son from cooling placenta.
They rushed him past his father, mumbled
words like *complications ...oxygen... stat ...,*
left him holding his sweaty forehead in both hands.

Life and Death on a Beach

We begin
this long run
toward the sand of shells,
dead chambers
of ragged claws
washed ashore, left
like treasure chests
to be picked up,
turned
and held up to the sun.

Leather bodies of old men
watch Geiger needles,
interpret clicks,
claw sand away
from bottle caps and toy cars,
drop brushed-off finds
into pouches
slung from hunched shoulders.
The young gray into ages
they hope for.
The glints of sea-breaks
lull them into believing
it will always be this way.

Meditation on a Heron

The white heat of a heron
rises from behind the fence,
long legs dangle
against a blue backdrop
after yesterday's storms.

The warm day has drawn him
to circle high over fish,
landscape folding beneath him,
including our own house and us.

Coffee steam rises today, too,
dissipates inches above mugs.
We gather beer bottles, empty
ash trays, sweep butts into the old coffee can,
hidden from the heron and houseguests.

The suburb hums alive
with trimmers and mowers
on a Florida late winter Saturday,
grass stretched upward after this week's
rain and a sunny afternoon or two.
Coffee makes the day normal.

Fish glide in low pools quickly draining
into humid air, unaware that the heron,
landing gear always ready, sways
in invisible currents overhead, listening
for ripples, watching for tiny splashes.

Fish is a better meal than lizards:
the heron will land, toss the fish into the air
like a clumsy, one-armed juggler,
lining up the fish head-first,
scales folded back against the body
to slide easy down his throat
in bursts of swallow.

And Just-Like-That She's Dead

Her heart stopped
like a watch wound down
to nothing.
She did not reject the liver
that flew across the country in a cooler,
racing against death, itself.

The surgeon trimmed it to size,
and the liver blushed with her blood,
swelled where it needed to be
"to be" whole again.
Her husband had parked on side streets,
lived in small chairs
in the waiting room or the corner of her room.
He watched the tabulation rising:
$1 million, more-than $1 million

for a life.

That life ceased,
and in the stillness of a moment,
the words lingered beneath
a Facebook throwback picture of him
and his recently-alive wife.

When I look up from the app,
the airport bustle of business travelers
and vacationers slows to a blur,
and no other moment matters-
the brain takes five,
stops recording,

and there's just
that photo,
the words,
and then
nothing.

New Year's Day

There is a silence
for the last one
      awake,
the one who pulls,
for the last time,
the plug that lights outdoors,
white lights lining the shape of the roof eaves,
candy canes, gumdrop lights
        encircling the tree out front.

Last night's fireworks
lie silent through a day
of quick football and leftover kraut
        and pork. Later, a pizza.
Maybe one last Christmas movie.

Pack away what's left of the tree,
bulbs in makeshift boxes, protected
by sheaves of Bounty,
lights wrapped carefully at first,
then quickly knotted into balls of cords,
cotton snow, shut wooden drawers of the advent tree,
ceramic nativity, all carefully arranged
to barely fit in the plastic tub.

The house returns
to an ordinary living room,
shoes kicked into the corner,
too many pieces of old mail
stacked on end tables,
no more green table cloth

or triangles of Christmas trees
on tea towels and decorative plates.

Guests drive into their own
sullen memories of this year—each
a re-memory of once-living ancestors
and the magic of some present
thought to be Santa-brought.

This year,
fewer presents, more talking, more repeating.
Those left in the house
get to the healing—the closing around
that heart—getting back
to the routine of school mornings,
the familiar soft glow of fake pine tree gone,
furniture all back in place,
no more spontaneous packages stowed
on the porch by busy postal workers.

You'll watch the few football games left
without parents, brother, or sister.
You'll eat
regular meals again: chicken and potatoes,
meatloaf and green beans, pork chops and apple sauce.
The eternal carcass of that ham, that turkey,
finally exhausted or abandoned,
casseroles scraped into garbage day.

There is a peace in the normal,
but there was a peace in the glow
of the 500 tiny bulbs draped
intentionally onto the synthetic branches,

a peace to sleeping in the kids'
room or the sofa so visiting brother can have a bed,
a peace to now-unfamiliar sibling bond,
familiar in the newness of how it happens,
intimate only until you were a team, now,
blood but little familiarity or likeness.

But what little is there becomes there
by the absence that looms,
the inevitable standing on the porch,
watching your brother drive away, back to work,
and you'll turn back into the life
you'd suspended.

I Want, Madly

I want to pound the cold stone
of a public bathroom wall,
my knees against my chest.

I want only one person
to carry me out of that room
into another room warmed by candles.

I want someone to help me
paste up magazine cut-outs
of eyes onto rented wallpaper,
eyes to watch and keep us safe.

I want someone to take away
the blade I use to sever myself
from the pills that make me normal.

Snow Day

When I reversed his coat
the sky opened
into a winter's lavender-small flakes
falling into a field where they become
one solid blanket.

He strained against the newness
of knee-high snow, too-big boots
held in place with snow pants,
heaving his small weight
against the resistance of snow piled on snow,
dragging the shiny blue sled back up that hill

beside the house. Mommy sets him again
toward Daddy who's waiting at the bottom
to catch him
before the whole thing
disappears
into the woods.

Winter Homes

silently through cold rain
birds fell
into a constellation
of wings
stretched taut
in wind
over the banyan

widows of long marriages
drive Cadillacs
into the breezes of US 41
between trailer parks
and early bird specials
at Picadilly Café

together soon
return home
silently

In Minneapolis

The cold people
crawl through glass skyways
peering into streets made famous
by Mary Tyler Moore.
I could live here,
crawling daily through tunnels
of glass suspended between buildings,
never leaving to feel the sun.
I could watch snow fall
onto frozen pedestrians
in ski jackets and earmuffs,
but I'm only here for the day.
I hope one day to return to this city
where music is piped through fake rocks
in the civilized spaces of fenced-in trees.
I want to eat Thai food
near the university
and spray paint my name
in orange letters on the tunnel walls.
People are just hurried enough
to forget that the Mississippi
is only a long walk away.
Nicolette Mall is a street,
and the mall of America looms
just outside the city.
If I lived in Minneapolis,
I would drive past farms,
like in my own Pennsylvania,
to Pine Island. I would dance
in the snow—colder than anywhere else
in this country.

Or else I would just walk
through miles of tunnels in the sky,
stopping to read books at Barnes & Noble,
buy a slice of pizza, watch a movie,
never stopping to look outside after a while.
Walk, as if in the apocalypse,
afraid to breathe in fumes and factory smoke,
afraid to expose myself
to the air or the public.

Teaching Again

Clouds tumble like bricks over the college.
Students lumber under backpacks
weighted with books, cell phones, and water bottles.
The light wind blows stronger. Water
drips from oak trees older than professors,
their canopy, higher than I can reach.
This summer, these students carry
sandaled feet over cracked sidewalks,
past the library, into some building of secrets.

When my brother started college
we drove him to a dorm—the stairwell smelled
like socks or urine.
I tried to dream of his classes
moving together into a new room
for math, and back again for English,
that he would line up, neatly among lunch-buyers,
after packers, and then those who buy milk.

I visit today, years after I began,
but this time I know where it leads.
These tired youth
forgot to read, so they hide behind the covers
of hard-backs full of equations, slouch
under questions, bleary eyes avoiding
the front desk.
When he walks past, a man in dreads
pulls a wrinkled schedule
from his back pocket, gazes against rain
at tiny plaques on brick buildings.

He wears a sweatshirt with the school's name,
like a mechanic's coveralls,
tells me he doesn't want to take
over his father's business.
He folds the schedule like a map
hiding it like success and fear
into the dark, denim recess
of his back pocket.
Tomorrow, he will read his map again,
or maybe he'll let the wind carry it away.

Big Shoulders

Blues crunch against smoky beer
ribs gnashed in crooked teeth
we order famous cheeseburgers
at Billy Goat's under the bridge
    a troll of grease
we cab to the suburbs
with a man
excited as we are for his first trip
to Mount Carmel Cemetery
we learn where the dead
lie
beneath untamed shrubs
against a large tombstone carved with sharp letters
C-A-P-O-N-E
smaller stones rest
like little heads
launching pads
for the souls of old gangsters
where ghosts rise
above the silence
of an undriven road
while the cabbie waits
speaking into the cell phone headset
in a language I can't hear
except as a rhythm
beside the orange cab
he waits for us
to finish springing between tombstones

like Spaniels
we return
the city rises
against the horizon
so small
so big

Fishing

Rooster tails, jig heads, and spinners sleep
in the green plastic tackle box.
I cast worms and crayfish
into silver shadows
swimming in the circle
of rigged fishing lights.

Sometimes a bass
vibrates the tip of the Ugly Stik,
or twenty inches of catfish drag the line
toward the middle of Kyle Lake.

If 6-lb. test line holds,
leather flesh glistens, tail swishes
slick patterns on the rock,
the fish croaks against moonlight.
I pin the piercing dorsal fin back,
wrench the barbed hook loose
and release him into a ripple.

Roots

I. Looking Backward

My family settled
into coal seams outside of the Alleghenies.
They worked until their bent bones collapsed
into the hillside graves I visit,
now only once a year.
The lime of their tombstones, melting,
lean over the narrow back roads.

II. Looking Forward

I think of the cemetery today
as I wait in the empty classroom.
New faces
sneak a smoke down the three steps
to the building side.
There, a banyan grown from a lost seed
grips a common palm tree,
spreading like fingers
from the veined wrist of a woman's hand
holding the stem of a violet.
The banyan reaches its tentacles into air,
where they sway in humid breezes
until they root in the ground,
become new trunks,
and the tree shifts its center.

What Remains

Driving the dirt roads to her home
      in the country past almost imperceptible

toads hopping through my headlights.

Staring at the sky
      from the acre of my grandma's 3 a.m. front yard.

One hand on my shoulder to steady himself,
      my grandfather points

his crooked finger
      to the stars he knew by name.

He primed the pump to draw pure water
      from the backyard well.

These memories of my grandfather recede
      into the valley behind the house

where the strip mine ponds dried up, where my brother
      killed his first deer,

where I poked into long, orange puddles at the jelly
      of frog eggs with a stick,

where I knelt to touch hoof prints
      left in clay.

Eventually, all I remember is grandpa
      scraping "deer guts" with a screwdriver

from the fender just behind the grill of his tan Nova.
        Still jolted from the impact, I wondered

whether the deer spirit would come back
        somehow to reclaim what she'd lost in our headlights.

That, and his "parrot finger" my sister named
        after he the beak of nail grew crooked

over the tip of his right index finger
        he lost to a lawnmower.

He is: a hand on my shoulder,
        accidental deer killer, parrot-finger. The man

who built this house when his father's new wife
        claimed theirs for her own.

In the expanse of the front yard just before snow,
        I lean my head back into interlaced fingers.

I can no longer point out the stars by name,
        but they're just where I remember them.

In the morning, I will touch the mighty black cherries
        and pines he planted as saplings.

Poem for Autumn

We crawl into the sumac jungle
    across the dirt trail.
        His tiny shoes kick through new-fallen leaves.

He fills his waiting wagon
    with hatless acorns, pinecones,
        dull shale stones.

I show him red maple leaves and yellow birch
    and tell him "it's autumn,
        when leaves are pretty."

Bristly pines brush green fingers
    against his cheek.
        Soon we'll make birch whistles,

heat-press red leaves into wax bookmarks,
    and hike far—to my grandfather's old strip mine
        where I learned to climb rocks and fish

for sunfish, where blackberries
    stained my own tiny fingers.
        This fall the grape vines hang bare

in the rusty orchard,
    maples crimson early.
        When I read him his bedtime story,

shut the window against cool air,
      he kisses me and falls asleep,
            and the only green left this year

glows
      from a very beautiful place
         within me.

Old Miners

They started scooping shale from the old mine again,
lifting light brown clumps from widening caverns.
They will load shovels of coal into the rusty boxes of dump
    trucks,
load dump trucks of coal into the riveted railroad cars
that lurch and squeal
South and West across the country.

The old dust settles again into drafty houses
near the old mine, the wives and widows
blow black into handkerchiefs.
Men blow black into paper towels
shoved in back pockets,
but they have a paycheck again

instead of first Friday relief.
With new shovels, the men plunge deeper
into the crusty ground, digging
in the same patch that's been dug for two generations,
always another layer beneath their fathers'.

My Own War

Hot blacktop underfoot,
each step reminds me
I'm still here in the land
of sand and lovebugs, palm trees
and retirees, my hands
raw with callouses
from the heat-soaked steering wheel.

What will it take to stop
lizards from flashing ruby throats
into unbearable sunlight?
The game continues as always—
warriors spinning their tails
like clock hands going out
of time.

Above Clouds

your voice drops
to a whisper   the storm passes
again

until needles of rain
knife   through my skin.

I walk the white cliffs

        of your smile.

This Guitar

balances on a porch chair,
waiting for the love of fingers
to pluck out the hunger
that hides inside,

waiting for my starving fingers
until I'm done with the day:
the lawn mowed, leaves scraped
from the gutters, spider webs swept
from secret corners.

It will sing
the way my friend taught me
to coax the melody out,
unsatisfied grumblings
of deep growls,
chords in the pit of my stomach.
I'll convince the siren
to sing her song
even if my own voice
falls flat.

In a Moment of Silence

Sweat streams down his thick neck
from under his black cap worn backwards.
Fingers silence the fat strings of his bass
just after a Neil Young tune.

He tries not to think of playing trailer chords
with his old band until his fingers bled.
The former lead singer sells aluminum siding now,
and the guitarist fills the spaces
between songs on WPSD.

These two remember
playing "Beer Nuts" and "Satan Escaped from Hell"
for fifty bucks and free beer
from a stale keg in a cabin.
They stole tabloid headlines for song titles,

sneaked cases of warm Heineken
past the drummer's father asleep
in a distorted, orange La-Z-Boy.
In Fred's lingering feedback

Bill waits for the next riff.
His fingers measure frets.
He cradles the bass and closes his eyes
against the brief darkness.

Occultist Oculist

I
squint
into charts
of letters blurred
against the smallest row.
The optometrist, occultist reads veins
veins in the back of my eye like
a broken egg, frowns
into my chart.
Then,
I
read
flashing lights
through the sides, peri-
pheral blur against the urge
to blink, my failing sight, the narrowing
world of glaucometric proportions
reacts to, restricts light in saucers
of eyes, dimming, darkening,
into one spot the size of a
yolk, sunny
side
up

Lavender Ink
lavenderink.org

www.ingramcontent.com/pod-product-compliance
Lightning Source LLC
Chambersburg PA
CBHW021407090426
42742CB00009B/1043